THE G.I. SERIES

· The War In Europe:
  From the Kasserine Pass to Berlin, 1942-1945

· Bluecoats:
  The U.S. Army in the West, 1848-1897

· Longknives:
  The U.S. Cavalry and Other Mounted Forces,
  1845-1942

· Billy Yank:
  The Uniform of the Union Army, 1861-1865

· Johnny Reb:
  The Uniform of the Confederate Army,
  1861-1865

· The War in the Pacific:
  From Pearl Harbor to Okinawa, 1941-1945

· Over There!
  The American Soldier in World War I

· The U.S. Army Today:
  From the End of the Cold War to the Present
  Day

· The U.S. Marine Corps

· Patton's Third Army

· Redlegs:
  The U.S. Artillery from the Civil War to the
  Spanish-American War, 1861-1898

· Sound the Charge:
  The U.S. Cavalry in the American West,
  1866-1916

· Fixed Bayonets:
  The U.S. Infantry from the American Civil War
  to the Surrender of Japan

· Grunts:
  U.S. Infantry in Vietnam

· Hell on Wheels:
  The Men of the U.S. Armored Forces, 1918 to
  the Present

· The Fall of Fortress Europe:
  From the Battle of the Bulge to the Crossing
  of the Rhine

· Terrible Swift Sword:
  Union Artillery, Cavalry and Infantry,
  1861-1865

· American Indians:
  In the U.S. Armed Forces, 1866-1945

· Custer and his Commands
  From West Point to Little Bighorn

· The Marines in World War II:
  From Pearl Harbor to Tokyo Bay

· Uncle Sam's Little Wars:
  The Spanish-American War, Philippine Insur-
  rection and Boxer Rebellion, 1898-1902

· Screaming Eagles:
  The 101st Airborne Division from D-Day to
  Desert Storm

Above: In 1873 the dismounted overcoat with a matching second cape attached for additional warmth was prescribed for all troops. It is possible that enlisted men of the Seventh Cavalry were issued this garment, but it is not known if they were. These were Civil War surplus garments that were converted to a new style but were only used for a scant few years until a new design greatcoat was produced in 1876, though it is also uncertain whether these were issued to the Seventh Cavalry. *USAQM*

Above: The well-dressed Seventh Cavalry enlisted man was to don a new dress uniform after major changes in pattern were prescribed in 1872. Old accoutrements of Civil War vintage, however, continued to be used in tandem with the new dress uniform for several years thereafter. *USAQM*

For this 8 October 1863 portrait Custer, as a recently promoted brigadier general of volunteers, wears the double-breasted frock coat with eight buttons in each row grouped in twos, as called for by regulations for officers of his rank. The collar and the cuffs were to be midnight blue velvet. The buttons are not the staff officer's pattern that were usually worn by general officers, but instead appear to be standard line officer's versions. The shoulder straps have gold embroidered outer borders and a silver star on a black or dark blue background. *NA*

Above: Gold galloons, additions of his own selection, ornament Brigadier General Custer's sleeves (far right) in this 9 October 1863 photo taken with General Pleasonton (seated beside Custer) and other Union officers, both regulars and volunteers, at Warrenton, Virginia. The officer standing in the center, First Lieutenant George Whitehead of the Sixth Pennsylvania Cavalry, has his sash 'scarf style' across the chest. This was correct for the officer of the day.

Most of the officers have elected to obtain short stable jackets, although the one on the far left, Sixth U.S. Cavalry First Lieutenant Benjamin Hutchins, has on a four-button sack coat. The first lieutenant standing behind General Pleasonton is George Yates of the Fourth Michigan Cavalry. After the Civil War he secured a regular army commission with Custer and the Seventh Cavalry. *LC*

Left: Captain Manning D. Birge of the Sixth Michigan Volunteer Cavalry has turned up the side of his slouch hat and added a pair of bars to the crown to indicate his rank, although he also wears the appropriate shoulder straps for this same purpose. *EGL*

Below: George G. Briggs, who ultimately commanded the Seventh Michigan Volunteer Cavalry under Custer, started his Civil War as a junior officer as seen here when he was a first lieutenant in the regiment. Note the regimental number above the crossed sabres cavalry officer's hat insignia. The hat itself has a lower crown than the regulation 1858 pattern. *EGL*

Opposite page, bottom: Brigadier General Custer's staff of the Michigan Cavalry Brigade depict typical examples of the varied uniforms donned by Union officers during the Civil War. Custer (seated, in front of the door) has added a single star to his civilian slouch hat and has a single gold stripe on the outer seams of his trousers, as opposed to the double gold stripes he wore on some of his other trousers after being elevated to brigadier general. The soldier in the left foreground wears the 1851-pattern mounted sky blue kersey enlisted man's overcoat. On the porch, Sergeant Michael Butler holds Custer's personal flag with white crossed sabers on a red upper and blue lower field. Butler wears the blue wool cavalry enlisted jacket with yellow worsted tape trim adopted in 1855. *LBBNM*

Right: Colonel Thornton F. Broadhead, commanding officer of the First Michigan Cavalry, wears the 1851-pattern officer's cloakcoat over his 1851-pattern field grade officer's double-breasted frock coat. *EGL*

Opposite page: As a major general Custer not only wore shoulder straps bearing two silver five-pointed stars, but also obtained a new double-breasted frock coat with nine buttons in each row grouped in threes, as called for by regulations for officers of that rank. Custer was named a brevet major general of volunteers in October 1864. *GS*

Left: William D. Mann, lieutenant colonel of the Fifth Michigan Volunteer Cavalry and later colonel of the Seventh Michigan, poses here in an 1851-pattern officer's overcoat worn over his 1851-pattern field grade officer's frock coat. *EGL*

Right: Custer's rank of major general was indicated both by regulation shoulder straps and his own addition of two silver stars (one of which can be seen here) applied to the crown of his broad-brimmed campaign hat. Note the cravat that was an optional accessory allowed by regulations. Usually these neckties were black, but Custer is also known to have had scarlet ones. *LC*

Below: Major General George Custer is joined by his wife, Elizabeth Bacon Custer, and his aide, brother Thomas Ward Custer, who appears with the shoulder straps of a second lieutenant attached to a tailored four-button sack with slash pocket at the breast. Note the gold general officer's hat cords that terminate in acorn devices on George Custer's hat. *NA*

Opposite page: A light blue shirt with broad collar having stars and piping applied, flowing red scarf, gauntlets, high polished boots, and a custom double-breasted frock with exterior pockets set off Major General Custer's wavy locks as he adopted the look of a dashing cavalier for this 23 May 1865 Matthew Brady portrait. *LC*

Left: The Third Division, (Sheridan's) Cavalry Corps, Army of the Potomac, adopted their division commander's red kerchief and a five pointed star above a Maltese cross in gold and blue as their corps badge. Here the badge is seen worn by Custer. *Museum of American History, SI*

Below: George Custer ('Autie') is joined by Mrs Carrie Farnham Lyon at Hempstead, Texas, on 18 October 1865. With the Civil War over, Custer now served on Reconstruction duty in the South. He has given up his former black slouch for a lighter broad-brimmed 'planter's hat' that was more suitable to the local climate. The lighter blue collar of his shirt, no doubt hand-made by his loving wife, continues to be worn over the collar of the dark blue specially-made major general's coat that was a shorter version than the regulation style, this example somewhat resembling a Navy 'peacoat'. *LBBNM*

Above: Custer put aside his slouch hat for a forage cap as seen in this November 1865 gathering at his Austin, Texas, headquarters. Wife Libbie and brother Tom are seated on either side of George, and father Emanuel (seated back right) is among the others in the party. The officer seated on the step at the right front is Lieutenant Colonel Jacob Greene, who has a modified field officer's double-breasted frock coat with seven buttons in each row, according to regulations, but has added an outside pocket midway between the chest and waist. He also seems to have a gold cord instead of the regulation leather chin strap on his forage cap. Note that Tom Custer has double gold stripes on his trousers, once again a departure from regulations and, as was often the case, mimicking his older sibling. *LBBNM*

Right: Major General and Mrs Custer appear in a more formal portrait, this time from September 1866, where both wear versions of the blue and gold badge adopted by Autie's cavalry corps during the late Civil War. They were at this time making the grand tour with President Andrew Johnson while he made his bid for election. *LBBNM*

Left: Lieutenants Edward Settle Godfrey, Francis Marion Gibson, and Edward Law (left to right) have on the typical garb of junior officers for the period when the Seventh U.S. Cavalry was forming in Kansas, during 1866. Godfrey and Gibson pose in the regulation 1851–72 company officer's dark blue single-breasted frock coat with nine gilt buttons, while Law has obtained a heavy double-breasted civilian jacket that seems suitable for campaign service. Law and Godfrey both have the officer's type *chasseur* forage cap with embroidered gold crossed sabers for cavalry and silver regimental numeral. *LBBNM*

Right: First Lieutenants James Montgomery Bell (left) and William Winer Cooke (right) pose on either side of Captain Myles Moylan in a view taken at Fort Leavenworth, Kansas *circa* 1870. All wear the *chasseur* style forage cap that would become regulation in 1872, as well as the 1861-pattern sky-blue wool trousers piped with a ⅛-inch yellow welt. The only other concession to military uniforming is Bell's fatigue coat. Civilian clothing otherwise predominates. *GS*

Right: In another image dating from the Seventh Cavalry's early years, Captain Owen Hale of Company K wears the company grade officer's nine-button frock coat with its stand collar turned to reveal the black collar lining and his large cravat. It is interesting to note that the *chasseur*-style forage cap is identical to the type that would be adopted as regulation in 1872, right down to the front cap insignia. The thin gold cord was typical but not regulation until 1883, leather ones being the prescribed strap before that time. Such deviations from regulations were not uncommon in the Seventh Cavalry or any other regiment serving in the American West after the Civil War. 'Holy Owen' was on detached service in 1876, but was killed the next year fighting the Nez Percé. *GS*

Left: A bemused Tom Custer peers down upon James Calhoun to his right and Thomas Mower McDougall, to his left. McDougall still has his infantry forage cap, having not yet replaced it with a new one after his transfer from the Fifth U.S. Volunteer Infantry to join the Seventh Cavalry. Custer has added specially made insignia with oak leaves, evidently to denote his wartime brevet as a major. McDougall wears the nine button company grade officer's frock coat. His light blue trousers are piped with the infantry officer's 1/8-inch dark blue welt. The trouser cuffs (bottoms) are kept in place by stirrups. Calhoun is in civilian garb, except for his officer's trousers. *GS*

Right: First Lieutenant Algernon 'Fresh' Smith displays an extravagant white cravat on his 1872 dress uniform, as was permitted for officers by regulation. Such deviations from the standard uniform were common among officers at the time, as any opportunity to demonstrate a degree of individuality was exploited to the full. *GS*

Left: In one more variation on the same theme Captain George Yates of Company F, or the 'Band Box Troop' as it was sometimes called, has obtained a civilian jacket with black frogs and fleece-lined lapels and collar, plus pockets as a functional winter field garment in lieu of the regulation frock coat or four-button sack. He has also selected gauntlets and high boots for field use, while the jaunty but less practical *chasseur* forage cap tops off this outfit of the late 1860s through early 1870s. The ⅛-inch yellow welt for officers can be seen on his trousers. *LBBNM*

Right: In another 'fashion statement' Yates has donned a 'pillbox' cap with crossed saber insignia and gold cap cord. Although such caps were non-regulation, their association with British officers serving in the far-flung parts of the empire appealed to some in the American military. Again a civilian jacket is pressed into service as a martial garment. *GS*

Left: Unlike in the other pictures, in this instance Yates wears the complete regulation full dress of cavalry company grade officers of the 1861–72 period, including epaulets. The coat is single-breasted with nine gilt buttons down the front, the sash is crimson, and the trousers sky-blue with an ⅛-inch welt let into the outer seams in yellow. Yates' cravat was an optional accessory. The 1858-pattern hat with two ostrich feathers for company grade officers and three for field grade officers was prescribed by regulations for dress occasions. It was to be looped on the right side and the brim on that side held in place by an embroidered 'Arms of the United States' device, while the front of the hat was to bear a gold embroidered crossed saber insignia surmounted by a silver '7' to indicate the regiment. Gold and black hat cords terminating in acorns completed this headpiece. *LBBNM*

Above: Captain Myles Walter Keogh of Company I wears a variation of the officer's 1858-pattern hat, similar to a style known as the 'Burnside hat', in reference to the Civil War Union general of the same name. The remainder of Keogh's pre-1872 outfit is regulation, although he wears his papal decorations in full size and miniature, as well as a XV Corps badge from the Civil War. *EL*

Above: Captain Albert Barnitz has set aside most regulation wear for his field outfit in this 1868 image. Only the trousers, crimson silk sash, saber, and saber belt are regulation, but the piped shirt, high boots, gauntlets, and plain slouch hat without insignia are typical purchased non-regulation items that were better suited for campaigns. *RMU*

Above: The Seventh Cavalry's early deployment was to various Kansas garrisons, including Fort Wallace where, on 26 June 1867, officers sat for a photo in front of the adjutant's office. Lieutenant James Bell (seated to the right) was the fort's commander. Bell's light cavalry saber is at his side. Also seen is Captain Albert Barnitz, seated in the center in a civilian style slouch hat favored by troops serving in the West. The remainder of the officers have the low crowned *chasseur* pattern forage caps that had gained popularity during the Civil War. To Barnitz's right an infantry lieutenant holds a Spencer carbine while the officer standing next to the door, probably First Lieutenant F.H. Beecher, Third U.S. Infantry, grasps a Henry lever-action rifle. Three enlisted men in the 1855-pattern cavalry jacket are also seen in the background, two with forage caps and a third with what is possibly the 1858-pattern enlisted man's hat with all the brass insignia removed. *YUL*

Right: His court martial over, Custer has been joined by family and friends for this group portrait taken at Fort Leavenworth, Kansas, in late 1867 or early 1868. Custer still wears his major general's wartime rank on the shoulders, indicated by two silver embroidered stars in the same fashion as they were placed on shoulder straps. His permanent rank as the lieutenant colonel of the Seventh Cavalry can be seen on the upper portions of the lapels of his civilian style 'Albert' coat, to which he has added insignia and what are probably gilt staff or general officer's buttons arranged as was regulation for a major general, two rows of nine buttons in groups of three. *LBBNM*

Left: Major Joel Elliot wears a field grade officer's frock coat with the collar turned back to expose the dark velvet lining. He has on the light colored vest (waistcoat) permitted by regulations for officers, and a necktie. Elliot would be killed at the Washita. The circumstances of his death contributed to a rift in the regiment. *GS*

Below: September 1869 found Custer, his friends, and fellow officers encamped near Big Dry Creek, Kansas, ostensibly to hunt buffalo. While the others are clothed in casual civilian styles, Custer relaxes in trademark buckskins with his newspaper. *LBBNM*

Opposite page: An impromptu officers' mess during the 1874 Black Hills Expedition reveals an officer in the foreground wearing the 1872-pattern campaign hat with broad brim hooked up and with his dark trousers carefully reinforced in the seat with a light-colored material, probably canvas. Also of note is his use of brogans instead of the more typical boots. Despite being far beyond the pale of civilization, the enlisted man in the background has on a white jacket befitting a waiter in an Eastern city's restaurant. *LBBNM*

Above: In the vicinity of the Little Heart River, a short ride from Fort Abraham Lincoln, Custer (center) and his favored officers relax during this July 1875 outing. Gone is the Civil War era look of the Washita Campaign, the officers now being seasoned campaigners and quite at ease in 'plainsman' attire. Custer's coat is the one rarely seen in photos of the era, while his nephew Boston (fourth from left) apparently wears his much used campaign buckskin. Note that Tom Custer (second from right) apes his brother's choice in headgear. *NA*

Below: Custer is bareheaded in this November 1873 group portrait taken on the steps of his quarters at Fort Abraham Lincoln, Dakota Territory, while both Captain William Thompson (leaning against the banister) and First Lieutenant James Calhoun (behind Custer) have on forage caps rather than helmets. In Calhoun's case the cap has a water-resistant removable cover. *SHSND*

In 1872 the 1858-pattern hat gave way to a new helmet for cavalry officers which bore the Arms of the United States in gilt metal with a silver regimental numeral superimposed on the shield. Custer has placed his helmet on a table next to him, and assumes the guise of a knight errant with his flowing plume, moustache, and long hair in this 1873 image. The outfit is the 1872-pattern field grade dress uniform of a lieutenant colonel of the Seventh Cavalry. The gold lace ornamentation on his cuffs is far larger than that called for by regulations of the time, the prescribed width being ¼-inch, but in Custer's case the lace is approximately ½-inch. Custer's manner of draping his gold chest cords is also non-regulation. *GS*

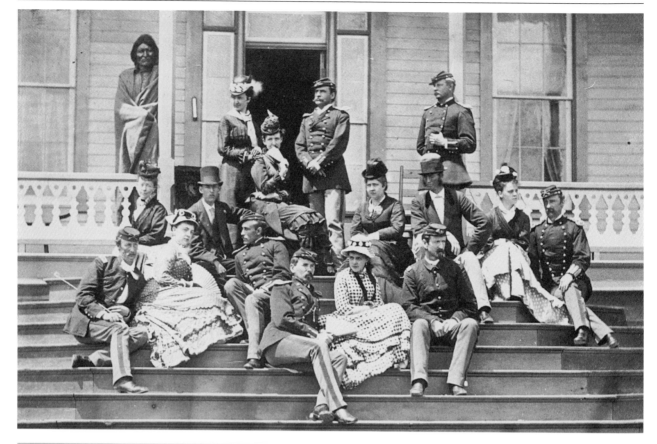

Above: This image showing the porch of Custer's quarters was taken in July 1875. Custer (seated far right) has once more removed his helmet, chest cords, and saber belt, and simply wears the forage cap with his dress uniform. Custer and many of his officers seemingly favored this combination for off-duty hours, as seen here. However, Tom Custer (far left first row) wears an 1872-pattern officer's fatigue blouse instead of the dress coat, as does Captain Stephen Baker of the Sixth U.S. Infantry (seated front row, right). Baker also wears the infantry hunting horn insignia that remained regulation until 1875 when it was replaced by crossed rifles. *LBBNM*

Left: During March 1876, while on leave in New York, Custer sat for José M. Mora. The coat is not the one Custer wears in other pictures, in that the width of the gold lace on the sleeves is ¼-inch per regulations rather than the wider lace he had sewn to his coat in earlier images. Did he purchase this coat in New York during this trip, or did he borrow the whole outfit for the photo session? The latter possibility seems plausible, especially in light of closer examination of the helmet by Custer's side. It bears a silver '8' not the '7' that was correctly affixed to Custer's helmet in a previous 1873 portrait, and is on his helmet which survives in the collection of the Smithsonian Institution's Museum of American History. *GS*

Right: Taken in April 1876, just a few months before his death, Custer again drapes his gold chest cord in a distinctive, non-regulation fashion. His field grade officer's gold lace belt with eagle belt plate can be seen, as can a portion of his Military Order of the Loyal Legion of the U.S. medal, a decoration presented by a veterans' organization in an era prior to campaign medals being issued by the federal government. *GS*

Left: First Lieutenant James Montgomery Bell, Company D, wears his dress uniform with the 1872-pattern officer's forage cap, a combination that was permitted for off-duty occasions. Officers frequently purchased caps with the insignia embroidered in silver wire bullion directly to the cap, as seen here. The rather thin gold bullion chinstrap was typical of a type that would not become regulation until 1883, although it was favored by many before that date. Note the white 'berlin' gloves and stiff detachable collar and cuffs. Bell was on leave of absence at the time of the Little Bighorn battle. *GS*

Opposite page, top left: Canadian-born First Lieutenant William Winer Cooke was adjutant of the Seventh. Here he has removed all indications of rank from his 1872-pattern officer's dress coat, having buttoned it open to reveal its velvet-lined collar and his white bow tie. The metal clips on his shoulder are to hold his 1872-pattern shoulder knots. Cooke was killed at Little Bighorn. *LBBNM*

Opposite page, top right: As adjutant Cooke wore a more complex set of shoulder knots than other officers in the regiment, the right one having an aiguillette attached to it. *LBBNM*

Above: Captain Frederick Benteen was pugnacious and stood squarely in the opposite camp from his commanding officer. He has altered a standard 1851-pattern mounted enlisted man's overcoat by adding a warm fur collar to this sky-blue kersey garment to provide an inexpensive field expedient. *GS*

Right: First Lieutenant James Calhoun of Company C wears a white cravat with a wing collar. Calhoun's shoulder knots have large rather inelegant 'paddles'. Calhoun was Custer's brother-in-law and was killed in action on 25 June 1876. *GS*

Left: Cooke's right 1872-pattern epaulet had the aiguillettes attached permanently. *Photograph by Gordon Chappell.* *CSPM*

Below: Detail of the end of Cooke's aiguillettes. *CSPM*

Left: Tom Custer, while still a first lieutenant, wears his two Medals of Honor, symbols of his valorous deeds during the Civil War, on his 1872-pattern company grade officer's uniform. Note the variation in the method of wearing his helmet cords. He would die alongside his brother. *LBBNM*

Left: Tom Custer wore his 1872-pattern folding hat *chapeau de bras* style in this photograph. He has the 1872-pattern officer's blouse with its black mohair frogging, but without the prescribed shoulder straps to designate his rank. The gauntlets bear a cryptic message 'K.O. 22d' the meaning of which remains a mystery. He holds an M1859 Light Cavalry Officer's Saber. *USAMHI*

Right: Company B's First Lieutenant William Thomas Craycroft sports a rather large black tie outside his stand collar. His saber is not regulation, and appears to be of European origin. The skirts of his 1872-pattern company grade officer's coat are also fairly short, as was not uncommon for mounted officers of the period. Craycroft was on detached service in June 1876. *GS*

Left: First Lieutenant Charles Camilius DeRudio of Company E was born in Italy. Sometimes called 'The Count' because of his personality and family background, DeRudio wears the officer's version of the 1872-pattern dress helmet. Minor differences distinguished the headgear worn by officers from those issued to the men, although variations from manufacturer to manufacturer existed as well. Shown here is the more complicated chinstrap of the officer's model. Also evident is the saber belt for company grade officers which was faced with gold lace interwoven with three silk stripes in the branch of service color, here yellow for cavalry, although appearing black due to the photographic process of the time. *GS*

Right: Here DeRudio has replaced his dress uniform with the 1872-pattern officer's blouse with the shoulder straps of a second lieutenant of cavalry. *BP*

Left: DeRudio was later promoted to first lieutenant and in this rank commanded Company A during the Little Bighorn battle. Here he wears the shoulder knots of a first lieutenant and has fitted himself out with an 1872-pattern officer's forage cap with correct leather chinstrap, as well as draping a cape over his right shoulder. He lived until 1910. *LBBNM*

Right: Lieutenant Winfield Scott Edgerly was one of those who saddled up and followed Company D's commander, Thomas Weir, on a pell-mell ride to locate Custer during the battle. Thinking better of this rash act, the men soon turned around and beat a hasty retreat to Major Marcus Reno's entrenched position to survive the battle. Edgerly has removed all insignia and turned back the lapels of his dress coat to reveal his studded shirt. *GS*

Left: Captain Thomas French of M Company has provided himself with a dark blue wool dress cape, dark leather gloves, and what appears to be an elaborate watch fob to accent his 1872-pattern dress uniform. *LBBNM*

Above: Here French appears with his 1872-pattern officer's forage cap, sans chinstrap. French survived the battle. *GS*

Above right: Company H's First Lieutenant Francis Marion Gibson wears a pair of fine gauntlets in this O.S. Goff image. Gauntlets were not issued to enlisted men until 1883, but most officers provided themselves with a pair. Gibson commanded Company G in the battle, and lived to 1919. *GS*

Right: First Lieutenant Edward Godfrey commanded Company K in 1876 and lived to a ripe old age, dying in 1932. The pronounced weave of Godfrey's bullion chest cord for his 1872-pattern dress uniform is typical of the 1870s. *GS*

Left: Company K's Second Lieutenant Luther Rector Hare could almost be mistaken for a civilian were it not for the officer's side stripe on his trousers. Officers were permitted to wear dark blue coats of quasi-military or civilian cut when not performing duties. Hare survived the battle and died in 1929. *GS*

Above: Second Lieutenant Charles Larned was one of the 'Custer Avengers' brought in to replace those officers killed at the Little Bighorn. His chest cords are draped upon his uniform in a haphazard fashion, typical for officers of the time. *GS*

Opposite page: Second Lieutenant Benjamin Hubert Hodgson of Company B wears the complete 1872 dress uniform as prescribed. Great attention was paid to the tailoring of these uniforms as evident by the fact that Hodgson's outfit is form fitting. He died at the Little Bighorn. *LBBNM*

Left: Captain Charles Stilliman Isley of Company E was an aide-de-camp to Brigadier General John Pope during the Little Bighorn Campaign, and thus wears an aiguillette on the right shoulder similar to W.W. Cooke's. His gauntlets are identical in detail to a pair owned by Custer that are now found in the collection of the Smithsonian Institution. Isley died in 1899. *LBBNM*

Above: First Lieutenant Donald McIntosh of Company G was not photographed frequently. Here he has on a forage cap instead of his dress helmet, a substitution that was permitted in those instances where officers were not serving with troops or carrying on strictly military duties. *LBBNM*

Left: Captain Thomas Mower McDougall of Company B shows the predilection for some officers to adopt larger, non-regulation sleeve lace. Also note that for this photograph he wears the tassels of his chest cord on the incorrect side of the uniform. McDougall survived the battle. *GS*

Left: Captain Myles Moylan of Company A wears the 1875-pattern officer's fatigue blouse buttoned only at the top, an affectation considered *de rigueur*, to reveal a pale vest and watch fob. Officers were permitted vests of blue or cream color by regulations. Moylan survived the battle. *GS*

Below: Second Lieutenant Andrew Humes Nave of Company I, seated in the center of this group portrait taken at Fort McKeen, Dakota Territory, in 1873, wears his 1872-pattern dress helmet and berlin gloves. The remainder of the officers are from the Seventeenth U.S. Infantry, and the diversity of their dress and campaign uniform demonstrates that officers of the 1870s tended toward a range of personally-selected outfits regardless of the regiment or branch. *GS*

Right: First Lieutenant Henry James Nowlan served as the regimental quartermaster at the time of the battle. Note the large cuffs of his stylish gauntlets and the medals he received from his prior service in the British Army during the Crimean War. *LBBNM*

Left: First Lieutenant James Ezekiel Porter of Company I strikes a familiar pose. Sitting on the table to his left is his 1872-pattern officer's dress helmet, an unusual example in that the plume base points fore and aft as opposed to the accepted pattern. This detail and the squat appearance of the helmet identifies it as one made by Baker and McKinney, a New York-based military outfitter. Porter was killed at Little Bighorn. *GS*

Left: Detail of a company grade officer's 1872-pattern dress saber belt lace from the *Annual Report of the Secretary of War* published in 1876.

Below: Second Lieutenant George Daniel Wallace was with Company G, but after the Little Bighorn he replaced Cooke as regimental adjutant, as indicated by the complicated aiguillettes that distinguished this position. *GS*

Opposite page: Captain Thomas Bell Weir of Company D sets off his 1872-pattern company grade officer's dress uniform with a pair of elegant thigh-high boots. Such footgear was more common during the Civil War, and recalled visions of romantic European cavaliers which so enamored many Victorians. *GS*

Left: In this view Weir has evidently converted an enlisted man's overcoat by the addition of dark astrakhan applied to the collar. *GS*

Below: Elaborate black silk galloons applied to the cuffs of the 1851-pattern officer's cloakcoat or capote were the marks of a general officer. Custer (front left) has also added non-regulation astrakhan trimming to the cuffs and collar of his overcoat. The other officers, Colonel G.A. Forsyth, Lieutenant General P.H. Sheridan, Major M.V. Ashe, Lieutenant Colonel N.B. Sweitzer, Major M.V. Sheridan, and Lieutenant Colonel J.W. Forsyth (left to right), likewise exhibit modified uniforms with elements of civilian clothing worn with military insignia, buttons, and other regulation accessories. Note the quatrefoil atop General Sheridan's forage cap. The image dates from around January 1872. *LBBNM*

Opposite page: The astrakhan addition to the collar of Custer's 1851-pattern officer's overcoat is also evident in this late 1871 or early 1872 cabinet card. Here he has combined civilian attire with components of the military uniform once more. *GS*

Left: Since ancient times, armies in foreign lands have adopted the dress of the local populace, an affectation declaring both supremacy and respect. So it was with the U.S. Army on the Plains. No single military figure became as identified with 'frontier buckskin' as the flamboyant Custer. In this 9 February 1868 photo taken at Fort Sill, Indian Territory (Oklahoma), a bearded Custer wears what would become a trademark campaign garment – a double-breasted buckskin coat. While superficially resembling an Indian shirt, Custer's buckskins were sewn, usually machined, by his tailor – a Seventh Cavalry soldier – and are patterned on the military styles of the day. Although he posed in numerous similar coats, Custer wore this particular coat on all his campaigns, and almost certainly on 25 June 1876. *LBBNM*

Right: This 1872 portrait, taken during a visit by Grand Duke Alexis of Russia, shows the same coat, this time being combined with Custer's trademark red scarf – a still potent symbol of his stature as a Civil War era icon. The modified M1868 .50-70 caliber Springfield rifle was one of several used by Custer's close friends at Fort Leavenworth, Kansas. *GS*

Right: Surrounded by his scouts (including Bloody Knife at his right and Goose standing behind his camp chair), his striker (or batman) John Burkman, and his prized hunting hounds, this 1874 image shows Custer again sporting a beard and his veteran buckskin coat. Featured prominently are a rolling block Remington rifle and two newly-acquired Colt Single Action Army revolvers. Note the four-button fatigue jacket worn by Goose. *LBBNM*

Right: Taken during the Black Hills Expedition of 1874, Custer's first grizzly bear kill is documented here, with the buckskin-clad Captain William Ludlow taking part in the photo session. Also present are Bloody Knife and Seventh Cavalry Private John Nunan (also known as Noonan, Nonen, and Nuwnen). Nunan wears the short-lived 1872-pattern pleated blouse while Bloody Knife has on the so-called, 'Fair-weather Christian' belt. Such cartridge belts were in common use long before the army conceded their utility and reluctantly began to issue them in late 1876. *LBBNM*

Above left: As evident in this *circa* 1875 picture, New Yorker John Briody, a corporal in Company F, opted to convert the roll collar of the old style four-button sack by adding what may be a velvet covering. He also had a convenient exterior breast pocket tailored into the blouse which he may have worn into the field at Little Bighorn, where he was killed.

Above: Private William O. Tyler of the Seventh U.S. Cavalry sat for the photographer in his 1872-pattern cavalry enlisted dress coat and 1872-pattern forage cap. All facings were to be yellow in contrast to the dark blue material of the coat. *GM*

Left: The Seventh U.S. Cavalry's regimental standard of the 1866–87 era. The cloth is of blue silk with painted Arms of the United States and survived the battle because it was stored with the pack train rather than being carried into combat. *LBBNM*

Right: This corporal of the Seventh Cavalry follows the 1872–81 regulations for dress uniforms. The long front and back visors of his helmet are evident, as are the regulation brass collar numerals which indicate his unit. Trim on the cuffs and shoulder loops is of yellow facing material, as is the 4-inch horizontal patch affixed to both sides of the collar. Yellow piping likewise ran around the top and bottom of the collar and down the front seams and along the skirt, which was slit at the sides for mounted troops. The horsehair plume and one-piece worsted helmet cords were to be yellow to match the chevrons, and ½-inch leg stripes were called for on trousers of corporals. *BB*

Left: The enlisted man's 1872-pattern cavalry dress helmet had yellow one-piece worsted cords and a yellow horsetail plume to match the trim of the coat. The collar was to display a pair of stamped sheet brass regimental numbers, one on each side, in this instance for the Seventh U.S. Cavalry. *MJM*

Opposite page: Sergeant Jeremiah Finley of Company C was among the many Irishmen who rode to the strains of *Garry Owen* at the Little Bighorn. A veteran of the Union army, he was a tailor as well as a soldier, and made the buckskin jacket Custer wore to his death, a fate which the sergeant shared. He appears in the 1872-pattern enlisted man's dress uniform. *GS*

Right: Officer's type brass snaps on his saber slings and the M1872 leather saber knot are two features of Daniel A. Kanipe's accoutrements. Also note the black japanned pinwheel ventilators on the side of his 1872-pattern enlisted man's helmet. *Montana Historical Society*

Left: Trumpeter Aloys Bohner, Company D, Seventh Cavalry, wears the 1872-pattern cavalry trumpeter's uniform, with its distinctive yellow 'herringbone' trim on the chest flanking each of the nine buttons of the coat. The gauntlets are privately purchased or a photographer's prop because these accessories were not issued to cavalrymen until 1884. Bohner was born in Germany. He survived the Little Bighorn campaign and remained in the regiment until his discharge in 1879, by which time he was the chief musician of the Seventh's band. *GS*

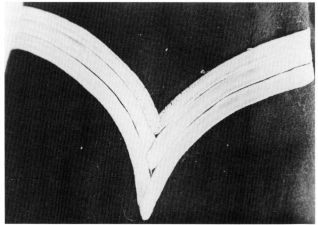

Above: Sergeant William William's dress coat has had custom chevrons applied, similar to those worn by other non-commissioned officers in the Seventh Cavalry during the 1870s. *LBBNM*

Left: Miles O'Hara, seen here as a corporal, had gullwing chevrons of yellow facing material, which while not issue, were typical of the early 1870s period and favored by some non-commissioned officers in the Seventh Cavalry. They were separately applied pieces of yellow cloth sewn on the sleeve of his 1874-pattern enlisted blouse, a garment that was to replace the previous pleated version. The yellow cord piping on the cuff of the jacket faintly shows in this image. Also note the three buttons on the cuff. Although the official pattern had only one button, the addition of up to three buttons was not uncommon. The 1872-pattern forage cap bears the old 1858-pattern cavalry crossed saber insignia. Finally, O'Hara has purchased a vest that is set off by a watch fob. *LBBNM*

Left: Trooper Korn holds Comanche, the 'brave horse', by the reins. The saddle is a leather-covered Jennifer type and sits on an officer's cheverac that typically was edged in yellow leather with a yellow leather numeral applied. Comanche was the mount of Captain Keogh and was wounded at Little Bighorn. Korn has on the 1874-pattern enlisted man's blouse and 1872-pattern forage cap. *GS*

All the privates in this picture have donned their 'walking out' outfits with a variety of individual touches. All wear the 1874-pattern blouse with the 1872-pattern forage cap, although the caps bear smaller non-regulation sabers in three of the four cases that will have been private purchases. The small brass company letters above the sabers are regulation size, however, as of 1872, although not until the middle of the decade did general orders clarify the manner of wearing these unit identifications. Also note that the man on the left, Musician George Penwell, has three buttons on the cuff of his blouse, rather than the one that was to be found on the specimen kept by the Quartermaster General's Department as the standard. In addition, Penwell has added double ½-inch stripes apparently applied to a piece of dark cloth and then sewn to the trousers. The practice of wearing double stripes finally became regulation for trumpeters and musicians in 1883, after many years of traditional use. *LBBNM*

Mora, Jose M, 40
Moylan, Captain Myles, 54

Nave, Second Lieutenant Adrew H., 54
Nowlan, First Lieutenant Henry J., 55
Nunen (aka Noonan, Nonen, an Nuwnen),
    Private John, 63

'Officer's Call', 8
O'Hara, Corporal Miles, 70
Order of the Loyal Legion, 40

Penwell, Musician George, 71
Pleasonton, Major General Alfred, 18, 20
Pope, Major General John, 52
Porter, Major General Andrew, 18
Porter, First Lieutenant James E., 55

Rifle
    Henry, Lever-Action, 33
    Remington, 63
    Springfield, M1868, 62

Saber
    Slings, 67
    Snaps, 67

Saddle
    Jennifer, 70
Sheridan, Major M.V., 60
Sitting Bull, 8
Smith, Colonel Andrew J., 6
Smith, First Lieutenant Algernon, 30
Stanton, Edwin, 6
Sturgis, Colonel Samuel D., 7, 56
Sturgis, Second Lieutenant James, 56
Sweitzer, Colonel N.B., 60

Tank
    755th Battalion, 29
Thompson, Captain William, 38
Trevilian Station, 6, 10

Wallace, Captain George, 8, 16, 58
Warrington, VA, 20
Washita, Indian Territory (Oklahoma), 6, 34, 38
Watch Fob, 14, 48, 70
Williams, Sergeant William, 14, 70
Wolverines, 6

Yankton, DT, 7